HARRY WOODBURN CHASE

HARRY WOODBURN CHASE

President of the University of North Carolina, 1919-1930
President of the University of Illinois, 1930-1933
Chancellor of New York University, 1933-1951

By

Louis R. Wilson

Chapel Hill
The University of North Carolina Press
1960

Copyright, 1960, by
The University of North Carolina Press

ACKNOWLEDGMENTS

FOR aid in the preparation of this sketch, grateful acknowledgment is made to the following individuals: Robert B. Downs, Director of Libraries, University of Illinois, for the loan of manuscripts of addresses delivered by President Chase, 1930-1933; Anthony J. Janata, Executive Assistant to the President and Secretary of the Board of Trustees, University of Illinois, for checking data; Mrs. Bernice Brightwell of Urbana, Illinois, for the use of a manuscript appraising the administration of President Chase by her father, the late Albert R. Lee, for many years Chief Clerk in the President's Office of the University of Illinois; Harold O. Voorhis, Vice-President and Secretary of New York University, for copies of addresses made at the testimonial dinner given in honor of Chancellor and Mrs. Chase on January 24, 1951, and resolutions of the Trustees and Faculty Council upon his retirement and death; Mrs. Ethel G. Martin, Archivist of Dartmouth College, for information concerning his record as an undergraduate student at Dartmouth; Howard B. Jefferson, President of Clark University, for information concerning his record as a graduate student at Clark University; Professor A. S. Chase, of Alabama Polytechnic Institute, for information concerning Groveland and its schools; and Mrs. H. W. Chase of Abington, Pennsylvania, for notices concerning special meetings of numerous educational, civic, and social institutions which she and Chancellor Chase attended in the Metropolitan area.

For statistical and historical information, use has been made of *The World Almanac, The Biennial Report* of the United States Office of Education, files of *The President's Report* of the University of North Carolina, the *Report of the Board of Trustees* of the University of Illinois, and the *Report of the Chancellor* of New York University.

Use has also been made of *The University of North Carolina, 1900-1930,* and the Addresses and Papers of Harry Woodburn Chase, in typescript, compiled by the writer.

Chapel Hill, N. C.
December, 1959

LOUIS R. WILSON

CONTENTS

Introduction	1
Biographical Sketch	2
The Background of Chase's Contribution to Higher Education	9
A New Englander at Chapel Hill	12
An "Adopted" Southerner in the Midwest	22
A Chancellor in a Metropolitan Area	37
Educational Direction for the Twentieth Century	50

INTRODUCTION

WHEN Harry Woodburn Chase retired as Chancellor of New York University in June, 1951, he had had the distinction of having served for thirty-two years as the President or Chancellor of three American universities. The institutions, their locations, and the periods of service were: the University of North Carolina in the rural agricultural setting of the South, 1919-1930; the University of Illinois in the stirring agricultural and industrial region of the Middle West, 1930-1933; and New York University in the highly complex metropolitan area of the Northeast, 1933-1951. He had also been a close student of higher education from his admission to Dartmouth College in 1900 throughout the first half of the twentieth century.

Chancellor Chase, however, had been much more than a student of higher education. He had both witnessed and participated in the tremendous expansion which higher education had undergone in the five decades that began with the period of relative calm following the Spanish-American War and embraced the outbreak of World War I; the turmoil on American campuses during the hectic days of the Students' Army Training Corps and the Armistice of 1918; the runaway boom of the 1920's; the eroding depression of the early 1930's; the frenzied preparation for World War II and participation in it during the first half of the 1940's; the unprecedented increase of students on the nation's campuses from 1945 to 1950; the "police action" in Korea; the onset of the cold war; and the mounting arms race for survival in the then-approaching space age.

Merely to have survived as the responsible head of three highly complex universities during such a soul-trying period was in itself a notable achievement. To have done so with poise, skill, and wisdom and to have given significant leadership to the educational movement of the times set Chase apart as a leader of the first order among American university statesmen.

BIOGRAPHICAL SKETCH

THE story of Chase's life in outline is fairly simple. Harry Woodburn Chase was born in Groveland, Massachusetts, April 11, 1883, the son of Charles Merrill and Agnes (Woodburn) Chase. He attended the local grammar and high schools in Groveland, a town of 2,376 inhabitants in 1900, and, in that year, entered Dartmouth College from which, after a distinguished career as a student, he received the degree of A.B., *magna cum laude,* in 1904. His record as an undergraduate was brilliant and marked by numerous scholastic honors. He

BIOGRAPHICAL SKETCH 3

was a Rufus Choate scholar during his junior and senior years; he received special honors in French and philosophy; he was a commencement speaker at his graduation, an honor given for excellence in scholarship for the entire college course; and he was admitted to Phi Beta Kappa, ranking fourth in his class.

Chase began his professional career as an educator in 1904 as a high school teacher; in 1908 he received his Master's degree from Dartmouth as a non-resident student, the title of his thesis being "Plato's Theory of Education."

Not content with his equipment as a student and teacher in the fields of education and philosophy, and attracted by the notable success of Clark University at Worcester, he relinquished his position as teacher in 1908 and entered the new, nationally acclaimed university to study under its distinguished scholar and president, Dr. G. Stanley Hall. Holding a fellowship in psychology, he served as the Director of the Clinic for Subnormal Children in 1909-1910 and later translated and published a series of lectures which had been delivered at Clark by Dr. Sigmund Freud, as a result of which the development of psychoanalysis in the United States was, according to Dr. A. A. Brill, decisively influenced.

His work at Clark was concluded in 1910 when he received the degree of Doctor of Philosophy in Psychology and Education, the title of his dissertation being "Psychoanalysis and the Unconscious."

Called to the University of North Carolina in September, 1910, Chase became a member of the faculty of the Department of Education, which later became the School of Education. First appointed as Professor of the Philosophy of Education, he retained that title until 1914 when he became Professor of Psychology and began laying the foundation of the present Department of Psychology. He took over the course in psychology previously taught by Professor H. H. Williams and introduced laboratory courses and scientific methods in that new and expanding field.

In addition to his duties in the departments of Education and Psychology, Chase served on a number of important committees, including the university Extension and Curriculum committees; and he was Chairman of the Committee on Intellectual Life. Following the death of President E. K. Graham in October, 1918, he was appointed Acting Dean of the College of Liberal Arts by Marvin H. Stacy, Chairman of the Faculty; and following Stacy's death in January, 1919, he was appointed chairman. In June, 1919, he was elected and on May 10, 1920, was installed as the tenth President of the University of North Carolina.

In December, 1910, he was married to Miss Lucetta Crum, a native of LaPorte, Indiana, and a graduate of Coe College, Iowa, who had been a graduate student at Clark University and had received the M.A. degree in 1910. At the time of his election to the presidency of the University of North Carolina, he and Mrs. Chase were living with their daughter Beth, aged six, in their home

BIOGRAPHICAL SKETCH 5

on East Rosemary Street, Chapel Hill, North Carolina. In May, 1930, before departing for the University of Illinois, President and Mrs. Chase adopted Carl Griggs, a university student from Winston-Salem, North Carolina, who took the name of Carl Carter Chase.

After serving the University of North Carolina with distinction as Professor and as President for twenty years, President Chase moved to the University of Illinois on July 3, 1930, and on July 5 was introduced to the university by retiring President David Kinley. He had been elected by the unanimous vote of the Board of Trustees on February 20, 1930, was settled briefly in Davenport House and for a year in the former President's House until the completion of the new President's House in 1931. He was installed as sixth President of the University of Illinois on May 1, 1931.

Coming to the presidency at Illinois at the depth of the depression, Chase met the situation resolutely, brought about an effective reorganization of the administrative structure of the university, liberalized student government, and illuminated generally the concept of what a modern state university should be. Although his tenure at Illinois was for only three years, he maintained the administration of the university at a high level and extended its structural organization by the addition of the colleges of Physical Education and Fine and Applied Art.

Elected Chancellor of New York University on January 23, 1933, he took up his residence at Washington Square and in July, 1933, entered upon his duties as the eighth Chancellor of that institution, a position which he filled with marked ability for eighteen years until his retirement in June, 1951.

During his career as a university administrator, Dr. Chase served as a member or officer of a number of educational associations. Among these were the North Carolina Education Association, the North Carolina College Conference, the Southern Association of Colleges and Secondary Schools, the North Central Association of Colleges and Secondary Schools, the National Association of State Universities (of which he was secretary-treasurer from 1922 to 1926 and president in 1928-1929), the American Association of Land-grant Colleges and State Universities, the American Council on Education, the National Education Association, and the American Association for Adult Education.

During his presidency and chancellorship, Dr. Chase had the unusual distinction of having the University of North Carolina and New York University admitted to membership in the Association of American Universities in 1922 and 1949, respectively.

Various educational and other foundations and organizations availed themselves of his services as a member of their boards of trustees or directors. Among these were: the Phelps-Stokes Fund, the General Education Board, the Julius Rosenwald Fund, the Russell Sage Foundation, the New York Public Library, the Metropolitan Opera Association, the New England Society of New York, the Chicago Century of Progress Exposition, and Town Hall.

BIOGRAPHICAL SKETCH

He also served as the Honorary President of the American Society of the French Legion of Honor, Honorary President of the Lotus Club of New York, President of the New York Academy of Public Education, Honorary Vice-President of the National Municipal League, and Honorary Vice-President of the New York Museum of Science and Industry.

A member of Sigma Nu social fraternity, Dr. Chase was also a member of various scholarship societies, including Phi Beta Kappa, Sigma Xi, Kappa Delta Pi, Psi Chi, Alpha Delta Sigma, and Beta Gamma Sigma. He served a term as President of Phi Beta Kappa Alumni in New York, the pioneer alumni chapter of the fraternity which was responsible for the establishment of the united chapters. His clubs included the University, Century, Bankers, Lawyers (New York City), Church, Town Hall, and Lotus. He was also a member of the vestry of Trinity Church.

The University of Oregon and the Social Science Research Council sought him as president during his stay at North Carolina, and the following colleges and universities conferred honorary degrees upon him: LL.D. from Lenoir-Rhyne College, 1920; Wake Forest College, 1920; University of Georgia, 1923; Dartmouth College, 1925; University of North Carolina, 1930; University of Michigan, 1932; Lafayette College, 1934; Franklin and Marshall College, 1937; New York University, 1951; L.H.D. from Rollins College in 1931; and a Litt.D. from Columbia University in 1934. Other honorary awards included the Chevalier of the French Legion of Honor, the King Christian X Medal (Denmark) of the Liberation of World War II, Commander of the Brazilian Order of the Southern Cross, and Officier de la Couronne de Chene of the Grand Duchy of Luxembourg.

In December, 1950, Chancellor Chase informed the governing Council of New York University that he considered it desirable that he relinquish his administrative duties. He was granted terminal leave of absence effective January 1, 1951, which continued until his retirement as of June 30, 1951. On January 24, 1951, he and Mrs. Chase were honored at a testimonial dinner given at the Waldorf-Astoria Hotel by the Federation of the Alumni of the University, attended by a company of 1,000 notable educators and leaders in many forms of educational, professional, and public life. The principal addresses of the occasion were made by Vice Chancellor LeRoy E. Kimball of New York University, an administrative colleague of Chase's; President Lawrence Fertig of the New York University Alumni Federation; and Dr. Oliver C. Carmichael, then President of the Carnegie Foundation for the Advancement of Teaching.

Following his retirement in 1951, Chancellor and Mrs. Chase spent their summers at their cottage at Northport, Long Island, and their winters in Sarasota, Florida, where in 1954 they established their home. Chancellor Chase died at his Florida home from a cerebral hemorrhage on April 20, 1955, at the age of 72. He was survived by Mrs. Chase; his daughter, Mrs. Marion Stone; his son, Carl

Carter; and a grandson, Harry Stone. Mrs. Stone died in 1957.

THE BACKGROUND OF CHASE'S CONTRIBUTION TO HIGHER EDUCATION

THE nature of Chase's contribution to higher education can best be understood by viewing it against the background of what occurred in that field during the first eventful half of the twentieth century. As has already been indicated, it was a period of unprecedented growth and abrupt changes incident to peace and war, prosperity and depression, and reconstruction in a world that moved from one major crisis after another to the climax which the nations are now facing at what it may be hoped is the peak and peaceful end of the cold war.

In 1900, when Chase entered Dartmouth, the tremendous transformation which he was to observe and to which he was to contribute was just beginning. Dartmouth had been founded as a colonial college in 1769 and had acquired a century and a third of tradition. Its characteristics in 1900 were those of the best liberal arts colleges of that day. Its curriculum stressed the classics and mathematics. It had made limited provision for the sciences and modern languages. The social sciences were being introduced; and, following the lead of Harvard, the curriculum had attained a degree of flexibility through electives. Medical courses taught by local physicians had been added early in the nineteenth century and, at the beginning of the twentieth century, courses in business administration had been added. The Dartmouth of his day was characterized by a carefully selected faculty that contained a number of distinguished members, a homogeneous student body of more than average ability, an unusually large library of 85,000 volumes, a recently established chapter of Phi Beta Kappa, a number of scholarships for students of distinction, an endowment of $2,500,000, and literary societies that competed successfully with fraternities for the extra-curricular time of the students.

The contrast between the status of higher education in 1900 and 1950 may be illustrated in several ways. All colleges and universities of the former date enrolled a total of 237,592 students; they were staffed by 23,868 faculty members; and they awarded 1,583 Master's degrees and 382 Ph.D. degrees, respectively. Harvard led the enrollment with 4,067 students, and Dartmouth and the three institutions of which Chase later became the principal administrative officer had student bodies as follows: Dartmouth, 752; North Carolina, 633; Illinois, 2,250; and New York University, 1,735. Total university and college enrollment for 1949-1950 was 2,659,021; faculty members, 246,722; Master's degrees, 58,183; Ph.D. de-

BACKGROUND OF HIS CONTRIBUTION 11

grees, 6,633; and the total number of colleges, including junior colleges which had developed in the first half of the century, numbered 1,851. The enrollment of Harvard was 11,175; Dartmouth, 2,939; North Carolina, 7,419; Illinois, 28,339; and New York University, 60,709 (summer school excluded).*

The number of volumes in the libraries of the four institutions named showed similar growth. Total volumes for Harvard in the two years mentioned were 525,000 and 5,397,286; for Dartmouth, 85,000 and 666,443; for North Carolina, 35,000 and 557,189; for Illinois, 50,000 and 2,383,503; and for New York University, 49,945 and 888,181.**

Total educational expenditures excluding capital outlay and income from auxiliary services showed a corresponding growth and tremendously expanded physical plants. Endowment followed a similar pattern, with 217 institutions having productive funds above $2,000,000 in 1949-1950, and those of Harvard reaching $190,000,000. Funds for university research, now running into the hundreds of millions, were also all but unknown, and publication by university presses was relatively in its infancy.

Johns Hopkins, the first American university developed

* Data are from the *World Almanac*, 1900, and the United States Office of Education *Biennial Survey*, 1948-1950. The data for New York University enrollments are for day and night and part-time as well as full-time students. They do not represent full-time equivalents. The number of full-time and part-time students was usually about the same.

** In 1950-1951 the number of volumes for New York University was 927,557.

along German university lines, had been established in 1876 and Stanford and Chicago had begun instruction in 1891 and 1892, respectively. Harvard had begun to modify its program in accordance with the emerging concept, but it still placed its emphasis largely upon Harvard College. The great expansion of institutions with which the nation is now familiar had been only dimly, if at all, foreseen.

It is against this background and that of World War I, the depression, and mounting world tension that the significance of the part played by Chancellor Chase is to be seen in its true perspective. His work, consequently, can be most fittingly summarized as that of the principal administrative officer at the University of North Carolina, the University of Illinois, and New York University, as an officer or member of the boards of directors of notable American educational associations, foundations, and other cultural organizations, and as a gifted speaker and writer concerning many aspects of education.

A NEW ENGLANDER AT CHAPEL HILL

ALTHOUGH Chase was a native New Englander, he quickly adapted himself to the environment of North Carolina and identified himself completely with

AT CHAPEL HILL 13

the interests of the university. His connection with the Division of Extension and the School of Education brought him into intimate contact with the educational situation in all parts of the state, and his relationship with students and colleagues in the faculty gave him a clear understanding of North Carolina attitudes and ambitions. His training enabled him to view these attitudes and ambitions objectively and to utilize his varied abilities to the best advantage in dealing with them.

Projected into the Acting-Deanship of the College of Liberal Arts and the Chairmanship of the Faculty by the tragic deaths of President Edward Kidder Graham (in October, 1918) and Dean Marvin H. Stacy (in January, 1919), he quickly demonstrated his ability as a wise administrator and was chosen President of the University at the June meeting of the Board of Trustees in 1919.

The objectives to which he devoted his principal attention in the eleven years of his presidency were: the establishment of the office of Dean of Students; the transfer of the responsibility of supervising discipline under the honor system from the office of the Dean of the College of Liberal Arts to a committee of the faculty and the Student Council; the reorganization of the entire administrative structure of the university through provision of administrative boards to formulate policies and advise the deans and officers of the principal units; the appointment of Mr. William Mitchell Kendall, of the New York firm of McKim, Mead, and White, as Consulting Architect to develop plans for the immediate and future expansion of the physical plant of the university and to add to the natural charm of the campus the beauty of architectural form; the addition of twenty-one new buildings and the very extensive modification of three other buildings to accommodate a student body of 3,000; the increase of the faculty from 78 to 225 members and the annual support of the University from $270,097 in 1918-1919 to $1,342,774 in 1928-1929; the staffing of professional schools with faculty members trained and experienced in professional education and administration instead of from the ranks of professional practitioners; the adoption of national instead of state or regional standards of scholarship and attainment; the defense of academic freedom and the right to teach science against the nation-wide fundamentalist crusade to outlaw the teaching of evolution; the establishment of new departments of Dramatic Art, Music, Journalism, Psychology, and Sociology, and schools of Business Administration, Public Welfare, and Library Science; the thorough reorganization of the Graduate School for training teachers and professional experts; the building up of a strong central library for the support of research; and the establishment of the widely known Institute for Research in Social Science and the University of North Carolina Press.*

Chase's first administrative act, the division of the duties of the office of the Dean of the College of Liberal

---

* These developments are treated at length in Louis R. Wilson's *The University of North Carolina, 1900-1930*. Chapel Hill: The University of North Carolina Press, 1957.

Arts, grew out of a crisis in student morale. Student self-government under the honor system had been almost completely wrecked during the military administration of the Students' Army Training Corps in the autumn of 1918. Both the military and academic programs of the university were placed largely in the hands of a commanding officer and second lieutenants who knew little about academic administration. The nation-wide influenza epidemic, the armistice, and demobilization all took place during this time; and the deaths of President Graham and Chairman of the Faculty Stacy cut even more deeply into university spirit and tradition. To meet this situation, former students were urged to return to the university as quickly as they were discharged, to help restore student self-government, and the functions of the office of the Dean of the College of Liberal Arts were divided because Chase was convinced that under the unusual circumstances prevailing, the responsibility for the formulation and execution of academic policies and for the direction of student life called for different approaches; each demanded the full time and thought of a gifted, single officer. He, therefore, established the office of Dean of Students to direct student life.

Another matter that severely tested his academic leadership was that of establishing the principle of staffing professional schools with faculty members not only professionally trained, but also experienced in professional teaching and administration. The test came in 1923 in the appointment of a dean of the Law School. The trustees, a majority of whom were lawyers, thought the deanship should be filled by a distinguished practitioner. Consequently, they proposed the names of a number of attorneys and present or former judges of the superior and supreme courts of North Carolina to fill the position. By proceeding slowly and by carefully studying the prevailing practice in the leading law schools of the country, Chase established convincingly the fact that the point of view held by the Trustees had been largely outmoded and that graduate training in law coupled with experience in teaching and in legal education was generally considered fundamental to successful administration and the building up of an effective program in that field. The establishment of this principle, in this instance, eliminated opposition to later appointments in other professional subjects.

The establishment of the Department of Sociology and the Institute for Research in Social Science likewise called for long and diplomatic handling. Sociology was generally suspect in the South, not so much by churchmen as by industrialists and politicians. The definitions of sociology and socialism in much of the region were identical. Both were horrendous subjects, and the less there was of them, the better. Chase moved unhurriedly in the matter; secured the acceptance in principle of the idea of establishing a Department of Sociology; then selected his Clark University fellow student, Howard W. Odum, a native Georgian serving as Dean of the College of Liberal Arts of Emory University—seemingly a safe background for filling the position—whom he some time later placed at the head of the department. The organization of the Institute for Research in Social Science followed two years later, the undertaking having received the aid and blessing of the Southern Division of the American Red Cross and financial support for five years from the Laura Spelman Rockefeller Memorial Foundation.

Provision of funds to build up the physical plant and faculty to accommodate a student enrollment of 3,000 after World War I posed another major difficulty. A newly created Budget Commission and the General Assembly of 1921 had to be convinced of the necessity. To carry his point, Chase launched a state-wide campaign, not only for the university, but for other state institutions which resulted in the passage of what became known as the Twenty Million Dollar Bond Issue. This action by the university and the General Assembly was unprecedented in North Carolina, and through it the university and other state institutions obtained over a six-year period the funds necessary for their very extensive expansion. The further action of the General Assembly in issuing $50 million of bonds for good roads sharply broke with the state's past attitude towards expenditures for badly needed services and contributed tremendously to its advance in higher education and in its total economic and social well being.

The most difficult objective to attain, or that which occasioned the most prolonged fight to secure its attainment, was that of freedom to teach and publish. While

Chase had spoken eloquently to students on various occasions about academic freedom and the search for truth and had emphasized the necessity for the university to maintain an atmosphere of intellectual honesty conducive to them, he gave concrete evidence of his strong devotion to these ideals in two critical instances. In 1925 and again in 1927 he fearlessly opposed fundamentalist-inspired measures pending in the General Assembly to restrict the teaching of evolution in state-supported institutions. At the same time he stoutly defended freedom of speech and the right to publish from an attack by the Presbyterian Synod of North Carolina on the publication of certain lectures delivered on the McNair Foundation on religion and science and on two scientific, sociological articles which appeared in *Social Forces*. His opposition to the proposed legislation, made in the House of Representatives of the General Assembly and in the state press and strongly supported by the faculty and trustees of the university and by other educational leaders, turned back the advocates of "monkey bill" legislation in North Carolina and contributed significantly to the reduction of similar threats to higher education in the region.

These were the major administrative tasks to which President Chase devoted his splendid training, his skilled direction, and his sound judgment in the eleven years of his presidency, during which the university was admitted to the Association of American Universities (1922) and was recognized throughout the academic world as an institution of high scholarly attainment.

But President Chase is remembered by the university for many other qualities and characteristics he exhibited as an individual during his Chapel Hill days. A tall man, with ruddy complexion and prematurely gray hair, an interested and excellent listener, he moved with ease and dignity among the members of the university community and enjoyed the affection and esteem of everyone. Singularly devoid of pretense, he was ever himself under all circumstances. He was at home with the man on the street as well as with the man in the cloister. Two other characteristics notably contributed to his administrative effectiveness and personal charm. In dealing with different problems, whether administrative or personal, he always based his decisions on principle and tempered them with unfailing courtesy and understanding.

The Faculty Committee, charged with drafting a memorial in his honor following his death in 1955, spoke feelingly of his place in the community and the larger community of university visitors, many of whom experienced the hospitality of his home. To quote the memorial:

"He was *par excellence* a faculty president. He knew and used every means of faculty participation in all processes of decision. The Faculty Building Committee worked with assurance and enthusiasm, knowing that their advice was decisive. Dr. Chase knew how to exert exactly the right persuasion at the right time with the Trustee members of the Building Committee. For he was *par excellence* a Trustee president. In the same way he guided faculty ideas about departments and schools to a wholesome point of agreement by the Trustees. Finally, he was *par excellence* an ideal student president, knowing how to keep students in participation through his Dean of Students and his faculty committees.

"It was in this family circle of students, faculty, and trustees that Dr. Chase was privileged to lead. His principle was to do nothing himself if he could possibly find some member of the University family who would take and keep the initiative. To such a man he gave full authority, full responsibility and full freedom. He looked for results but he measured these against universal standards. The result was that every person on the staff from the lowest in rank to the highest felt a sense of gusto, personal and professional progress while the University moved increasingly into larger activities and rose to higher achievements. Under his direction the University was, to use a Navy expression, "a happy ship." Dr. Chase had the rare ability to listen to the clashing ideas and wills of strong and ambitious persons and to come up at the right moment with a formula on which all could agree. This was his genius and it was one ingredient in his success in his office, both here and elsewhere.

"Another role of Dr. Chase's which stands out vividly in the minds of his contemporaries was that of host to the University's distinguished guests. Before the opening of the Carolina Inn in nineteen twenty-four, Dr. and Mrs. Chase entertained many of the important visitors who came to the University. Cabinet members, governors, college presidents, commencement speakers and recipients of honorary degrees, as well as distinguished lecturers and scholars, enjoyed the delightful hospitality of their home. Members of the faculty here were also frequent guests, and Mrs. Chase's keen interest in the social and artistic life of the community made her home a center of activities and brilliant social gatherings. In the president's files are many letters showing the delight and appreciation of visitors in the Chase home; and this wide reputation for friendliness and hospitality was one of the many factors which made a strong and favorable impression on friends and alumni of the University."

This appreciation by visitors of the charm and warm friendliness of the Chase home at "The President's House" at Chapel Hill was also felt by guests at "The President's House" at Urbana and "The Chancellor's House" at Washington Square. All, alike experienced a gracious hospitality that remained for them a singularly treasured memory.

AN "ADOPTED" SOUTHERNER IN THE MIDWEST

DR. Chase transferred to the University of Illinois in July, 1930, and on July 5 assumed the duties of the presidency relinquished by his predecessor, President David Kinley. Called to take over the administration of this great midwestern university, then at a high stage of development and commanding influence within the state and nation, Chase looked forward to a period of distinguished achievement. A native of New England, who had become an "adopted" southerner, an administrator who had had nine years of experience as a university teacher and eleven as a skilled administrator, he entered upon his duties with high expectation as the university's sixth president. The enrollment of the university in 1929-1930 was 13,370; it had a fine faculty including a number of unusually distinguished members, and its appropriation from the state for the biennium was $12,030,-000, with funds from the preceding biennium for the completion of several previously projected buildings.

The internal administration of the university claimed Chase's first attention. He found the Council of Administration, composed of the President and deans, meeting weekly and spending valuable time upon matters many of which were of relatively small importance. This limited the time that could be given to policy making and to the consideration of matters of larger moment. Profiting from his experience at North Carolina where he had completely reorganized the administrative structure, he secured the dissolution of this Council and replaced it with a University Council whose activities were concerned with matters of major university importance. He also followed the pattern set at North Carolina in dealing with the problems of student discipline. He relieved the deans of men and women of the duties of administering discipline and assigned that function to a faculty committee, leaving it to the deans of men and women to serve as student advisors. He also secured the appointment of a Provost to assist the President in the administration of the educational and financial programs and sought the appointment of two or three general administrative officers with responsibility for large areas of administration. In this move, however, he was unsuccessful on account of the deepening depression. But by the addition of the Provost and by changing the duties of his administrative assistant in such a way as to relieve the President of certain responsibilities, he effected a reorganization of the President's office that greatly increased its general effectiveness.

Other administrative changes were made. One was the formation of the College of Fine and Applied Arts (in 1931) by bringing together the departments of Architecture, Art, a new Department of Landscape Architecture (formerly a division of the Department of Horticulture), and the School of Music. Another was the formation of the School of Physical Education in 1932 through the reorganization of the Department of Physical Welfare which included the departments of physical education for men and women and the University Health Service.

Student government, however, was an area of university activity to which Chase gave immediate and special attention. Having separated the duties of advising students from those of disciplining them in the offices of the Dean of Men and Dean of Women and having appointed a faculty committee to administer discipline, he sought the liberalization of the regulations governing students. In an early address to the students he suggested that they should assume greater responsibility for their own direction. A committee of students drawn from various parts of the university was formed and a significant amelioration of the rules was effected. *The Daily Illini,* in commenting on the eighty-page booklet containing the 138 regulations governing the students in 1930, quoted Chase as saying, "The only document I know comparable to our regulations for the conduct of undergraduate students is the Book of Leviticus." The *Illini* went on to say that "by 1932 Chase had whittled it down to about 16 pages and 39 rules," an action that led some critics of the President to express the fear that he was undermining student morals!

The question of smoking also gave Chase concern, and his suspension of the tradition that smoking should not be permitted within certain areas of the main campus accentuated the criticism referred to above. *The Chapel Hill Weekly,* knowing of this tradition when Chase accepted the Illinois presidency, commiserated him as follows:

"The sympathy of all who know him goes out to President Harry W. Chase at the disclosure that he will have to give up his cigarettes when he goes to take command of the University of Illinois next September. The law there forbids smoking anywhere on the reservation—in the University buildings and on the Campus. Our community has been accustomed to see President Chase puffing on a cigarette as he saunters along the village streets or up and down the campus paths; and in his office in the South Building, when he prepares an address or struggles with knotty problems of administration, Lady Nicotine has been with him to give comfort and inspiration. Now he is to be robbed of her companionship at the dictates of the Middle Western rectitude. This seems to us a major tragedy. . . . It may be that public sentiment and the traditions of the University will permit him an occasional quiet smoke in the citadel of his home,—we do not know about that,—but surreptitious indulgence of that sort does not offer a pleasant prospect. When a man of 46 has for years been smoking whenever and wherever he pleased, with the full consent of his own conscience and the approval of the faculty, his students, his village, and his state, we should think it would be poor consolation to know that after a weary and smokeless day he could look forward to a cigarette after he had got home at nightfall and closed the door securely behind him." Following the "suspension," smoking was permitted in the offices and entrances of fireproof buildings.

Chase, a brick-and-mortar president at Chapel Hill, did not add materially to the Illinois physical plant. The three-year tenure of his office and the depth of the depression made this all but impossible. But he did add the following six buildings through funds appropriated under the administration of President Kinley, who had inaugurated a ten-year building program: the Chemical Annex, the Women's Gymnasium, the Ice Skating Rink, the President's House, the Water Filter Plant, and the first unit of the Medical Laboratory in Chicago. The Skating Rink was built out of funds provided by the Athletic Association in earlier and more successful football seasons.

While the foregoing changes were being projected and carried into effect, the formal inauguration of President Chase was held. The date was May 1, 1931, and the occasion was made notable by the presence on the campus of a host of representatives of the academic world, officials of the state and the university, and faculty, student body, and alumni. In his Inaugural Address, he reviewed the history of the university and projected its future in keeping with what he considered should be the pattern of development of state-supported universities during the mid-twentieth century. He saw such institutions as the instruments designed for the adjustment of young men and women to the inevitably complex and bewildering life of the future civilization. He insisted that these institutions must not be afraid to experiment with new ideas and must reinterpret and reassess their work in the light of their new obligations. He also projected the role of the University of Illinois in the new day. With its history of courage, vision, and devotion, he looked to it set "in the midst of a rich, changing, and growing empire, stimulated by its life and its problems," to "write a new chapter in the history of popular higher education in America."

The immediate realization of these hopes, however, began at once to be dimmed by the depression which made itself increasingly felt in 1931, 1932, and 1933, leading to a marked reduction in the university's appropriations, the elimination of funds for new buildings, a crippling cut in faculty salaries, and a drop in student enrollment on both the down-state and Chicago campuses. These financial difficulties were added to by others affecting the administration which, while they were less important, were more personal and disturbing to the President. As a result of the depression and the political unrest of the period, the Republican administration of Illinois was swept out of office in 1932 and was succeeded by a Democratic governor, a Democratic legislature, and three new members of the Board of Trustees who had succeeded three members who had become familiar with the complex nature of the university through several years of experience on the board.

Furthermore, the new house for the President, that had been authorized in 1928 and completed in 1931, had to be furnished. Since it was planned not only to be occupied by the President, but to provide facilities for the entertainment of university guests and the holding of various university functions, $43,324 was expended for the furnishings, with the result that the house, including landscaping and furnishings, cost $207,238. Although President Chase had had nothing to do originally with the planning of the building or the general scale of furnishings and had opposed a supplementary appropriation for furnishings included in the total, he and Mrs. Chase were improperly criticised as having been responsible for the expensive outlay. The matter was seized upon by a disaffected member of the legislature, and the state press played the matter up in a sensational manner that was most unfair and distasteful.

The new chief executive of Illinois, Governor Henry Horner, also insisted on a survey of university positions, functions, and salaries and named a Chicago company to make the survey, a company which previously had had but little experience in dealing with the peculiarities and complexities of university objectives and finances. The university was also unsuccessful in securing adequate state appropriations for 1933-1935, and the budget for that biennium was cut from the $10,075,000 for 1931-1933, which Chase had secured from a friendly governor and legislature, to $7,795,000. The closing and subsequent reopening of the First National Bank of Champaign in

1932, in which the university deposited its funds, also complicated matters, although the university suffered no loss of funds, since they were carefully safe-guarded.*

These financial difficulties were necessarily accompanied by salary cuts and the worsening of morale incident to lower salaries, declining enrollment, and the generally prevailing sense of insecurity.

The criticism concerning the change in the regulations governing undergraduates, the suspension of the rule concerning smoking, the parading in the press of the cost of the various furnishings of the President's House, and the critical attitude of the governor and the legislature, all bore heavily upon Chase and made extremely difficult the final six months of his presidency at Illinois. However, he carried on and saw the financial status of the university stabilized for the biennium 1933-1935 and the reputation of the university maintained at a high level. He had been confronted with severe financial limitations in North Carolina in the biennium 1929-1931, and he was well aware of the serious financial problems with which all American university executives were then struggling. These facts mitigated in some degree the difficulties of the situation and enabled him to bear them philosophically.

On January 25, 1933, while projecting the financial campaign of the University of Illinois for the biennium 1933-1935, President Chase addressed a letter to the

* These figures were supplied by Mr. Anthony J. Janata, Executive Assistant to the President and Secretary of the Board of Trustees of the University of Illinois.

Board of Trustees tendering his resignation to take effect July 1 following. He had been elected on January 23 to the Chancellorship of New York University and had accepted the position, the acceptance to become effective following the termination of his service at Illinois. The resignation was immediately accepted with appropriate resolutions, and on July 10, having completed the legislative campaign, he relinquished his work at a board meeting, to be succeeded by Dr. Arthur Hill Daniel, Dean of the Graduate School and Acting Dean of the College of Liberal Arts and Sciences.

An appraisal of President Chase's administration at Illinois is difficult. It was only three years in length in a period in which constructive planning and fruitful fulfillment, other than in matters of administrative reorganization, were largely impossible on account of decreasing funds. And even in the case of the administrative changes effected, some of them had to be carried out by individuals who may not have fully understood what President Chase had in mind or may not have been in full sympathy with them.

Several measures taken by President Chase, however, contributed greatly to the administrative effectiveness of the university. The replacement of the Council of Administration, an executive body, by the University Council, charged with advisory and planning functions, led to the immediate modification of some objectives and to the formulation of others from which the university would inevitably profit. The establishment of the College of

Fine and Applied Arts and the School of Physical Education led to more unified direction of the programs of those organizations, and the appointment of a provost to assist in educational administration and other reorganization greatly expedited the handling of daily operations.

Another change of an administrative nature dealt with the problems of student government and campus regulations. The separation of discipline from the offices of the deans of men and women, the assumption of greater responsibility by students for governing themselves, and the lifting of the ban on smoking under certain conditions were indicative of a positive rather than a negative approach to these problems. This was a distinct gain, even though it met with resistance in some quarters.

The above-mentioned changes affected administrative organization. From the addresses he delivered before university and other audiences, it is evident that Chase sought a clear understanding by students, faculty, trustees, alumni, state officers, and the public generally of the nature and objectives of higher education, particularly of state universities. Consequently, he dealt with aspects of this subject on numerous occasions.

Excerpts from his addresses during his three years at Urbana show what these objectives were. Speaking before the faculty on September 18, 1930, at the beginning of his administration at Illinois, he established the point of view that a state university had the definite task of raising the general level of education throughout the state that supported it. Although tens of thousands of young men and women who attended such a university would lead lives which might be relatively undistinguished, they would nevertheless have a better understanding of life and the role they should play as useful citizens. They would go out and serve in the ranks, but in a more intelligent and better disposed way. Coupled with this, such a university was also confronted with the task of training for leadership. It should discharge that duty intelligently and well amid all the complications that come from doing things on a large scale.

He further insisted that educationally state universities were young, that they ought to face their problems resolutely in their own way and in terms of the generations to which they belonged. They ought not to fear what was different, what was new, what was promising. Furthermore, they should be willing to experiment, not according to some fixed formula, but through a spirit of open-minded and scientific inquiry, whether the problems were those of liberal or professional curricula or organization of student life or in whatever field they happened to lie.

He also maintained that the immediate mission of the state university was not limited to the campus. Its service to the public, its extension work in agriculture and home economics, its activities in the fields of adult education were as much a part of its mission as instruction and research upon the campus. Throughout the entire university, it was supremely important to have a free and interested play of minds about the common problems of university education. Regimentation was not in the spirit of an educational institution. Free stimulation to inquiry, to creation, and to human advancement was of its very soul and essence.

Speaking again at his installation in May, 1931, to the faculty, the trustees, and the public, he declared "There are many old and well-tried fundamentals with which no university, however founded or maintained, can dispense and remain a university. There must be in all real universities a freedom to teach and investigate. There must not be interference from without in matters of control and policy that are properly within the scope of the university itself. There must be competence in teaching and research; the determination to press beyond the frontiers of knowledge; opportunity for the great teacher and the distinguished scholar. The State universities which have prospered and grown great are precisely those whose states . . . have had the wisdom to recognize these things and so to assure for them the maintenance of those conditions without which a university becomes but an empty name. . . . All attempts to utilize State universities for personal or partisan purposes have reacted disastrously both on the Universities and on the partisans. Neither can State universities ever conceive of themselves as the instruments of any class or party or creed or faction within the State."

One of President Chase's greatest concerns, however, centered around the ideal which students should acquire to fit them for meeting the problems of their day. He had developed this theme at North Carolina in two notable addresses to the students.* One dealt with the importance of their seeking truth relentlessly and with open minds. The other emphasized the responsibility of the university to surround students with an environment of intellectual honesty in which freedom of thought and discussion had full play. This conviction lay back of his insistence on changing the approach to student discipline at Illinois through a multiplicity of regulations to that of inner self-control. Speaking at the University of Chicago Chapel in March, 1932, on the subject of religion, he restated his position in these eloquent paragraphs concerning the truly educated man:

"It has been my business for a quarter of a century to be concerned with education. . . . I have come to hold very sincerely and very passionately one conviction. That is that one of the tasks which so-called higher education is called on to perform is to help people learn how to stand on their own feet. I have less and less patience with a multiplicity of rules and regulations and prohibitions and external constraints which it seems to me tend to prolong childhood dependence and reliance on external authority. Education ought to be something within the individual if it is anything at all. There ought to be enough determination in the individual to make him do some things for himself or he ought not be a member of a community which is devoted to education. He ought

* "Truth as a University Ideal," September, 1923, and "The University's Intellectual Responsibility," October, 1923.

to learn how to behave himself morally through a process of taking responsibility for his own actions and not by any endless network of exterior compulsions. If we fail in education in developing individuals who are able to take responsibility for themselves I think we have failed to grasp one of the points of what our education is about. How desperately today do we need citizens in this Republic whose actions are determined by the inward and uncompelled actions of virtue rather than by the outward constraint of law! The very heart of the problem of self-government, it seems to me, depends on whether we can strengthen the forces which make for inner responsibility and self-control.

"I have spoken in this in terms of education. I am sure you see my further point. For religion, like education, is something inside a man. I have tried to say that in my mind religion is not the same thing as theology; that it ought not be thought about in terms of social authority; but that the essence of it is the inner experience of the individual himself—an experience which makes him feel in harmony with the great underlying spiritual forces of the universe. If you believe, as I firmly do believe, in the importance of inner restraints and controls in this day when so many forces make for breakdowns in precisely these things, if as I say, you believe in these things then you will be on the side of the religious forces of your communities as they attempt, by varying methods and with different creeds, to accomplish this result.

"I have tried to talk to you as educated men and women about your responsibility to this great area of religion. I can but feel that in the confusion which so often exists as to what religion really is and means, in our irritation at the activities of some of its representatives, in our feeling that modern life has swung away from some of its teachings, we tend to confuse ourselves and to forget that after all it is the expression on one's self in a sense of harmony with those things which are greater and deeper than ourselves. In this sense the inward development which religion purposes is the development of a character of uncompelled virtue . . . through faith that there is reality behind appearance, through faith that there are in life spiritual values, in short that there is a cause of righteousness as there is a cause of truth."*

These ideas constituted the fundamentals of Chase's matured educational creed. Consequently, he presented them frequently to the university clientele and to the wider public of educational and cultural bodies and readers during the three years he remained at Illinois. Although some of the administrative changes, particularly those concerning student regulations, evoked sharp criticism, they and the ideas enunciated by President Chase made for the liberalization of university thought and increased public understanding of the role of the state university in American life.

Chase tendered his resignation with reluctance. Nevertheless, he must have welcomed the prospect of freedom from biennial struggles with legislatures (eight

* "Religion and the Educated Man," March, 1932.

in fourteen years) and of administration of a private university dedicated to the service of America's largest metropolitan center.

A CHANCELLOR IN A METROPOLITAN AREA

THE transfer from Urbana-Champaign to New York City, unlike that from North Carolina to Illionis, represented something more than the change from a smaller state university located in a comparatively small population area to a larger one in a more populous agricultural and industrialized setting. It was a transfer to a private, decentralized university spread out in various sections of America's largest metropolitan area and drawing its students principally from the immediate surroundings, which were unprecedentedly rich in resources of professional personnel, of cultural institutions, and of materials for study and research in almost infinite variety.

In his first *Report of the Chancellor,* Chase noted these characteristics and commented on the appeal that they made to him:

"The decision which brought me to New York was influenced largely by what New York University is and what it stands for. Its ideals and purposes are of a character that long before I came to know the institution appealed to me as sound. What I have discovered in the course of the past year confirms and intensifies that feeling. Those who kindled the flame of learning here a hundred years ago, and those who have kept it alive through all the intervening time, have staked their resources and exended their lives in furtherance of the principle that enlightened citizenship is a primary essential of democracy. Under no other form of government is unstinted educational opportunity so requisite. We need in this country the type of education that frees the human mind from ignorance and superstition, and loosens the bonds of oppressing circumstance. We need throughout our schools and colleges the type of educational training that not only gives each student the chance of development according to his capacity, but ferrets out native ability and encourages and stimulates intellectual aptitude, wherever it may be found, to the highest degree. Only by such thoroughgoing processes can individual talent be brought to the richest fruition, and the community and the Nation benefited in the highest degree. It is that kind of educational opportunity that forms the corner stone and permeates the whole structure of New York University. Its seine is cast boldly into the full tide of this vast metropolitan life. The surging throng of students that hungrily lay hold upon its facilities is no less cosmopolitan than the populace of the City itself. It is a fascinating, a thrilling experience, ministering to the needs of this amazing constituency."*

He saw a further challenge in the metropolitan area's educational problem. "Higher education in America," he wrote, "has the function both of training the individual and of raising the mass level. With the tremendously increasing popularity of college and university training, the function of raising the mass level has necessarily assumed increasing importance. Such popularization is essentially right. It reflects a deep-seated urge in American society. It points towards an enrichment of life for many people who will never achieve distinction. It promises the making of a better citizenship, and the training of a people more able to cope with the problems that confront them. While New York University, so closely integrated with the life of the metropolitan area, has necessarily been obedient to the cause of raising the mass level, it has at the same time fostered and encouraged individual progress and achievement to the limit of its resources. It is a problem of every university where to lay emphasis between these two functions. Each institution must play its own role. The two functions are not incompatible. The history of the State universities seems to me to indicate that there is no fundamental contradiction between the large scale accomplishment in popular education and the assiduous training of outstanding individuals on a high qualitative level, no inconsistency, but plenty of difficulty. How can we best do this? How can we best develop departments doing work of greater dis-

* New York University *Report of the Chancellor*, 1933-1934, pp. 1-2.

tinction and at the same time carry forward on a broad basis? This University, at all events, is committed to the effort. It was the provocative character of this extraordinary situation that attracted me."*

Comfortably settled in a delightful two-story detached brick house at 2 Fifth Avenue, in the shadow of Washington Square, which served as the Chancellor's House for a few years,** Chancellor Chase began his administration of this institution that only a year before had celebrated its one hundredth anniversary. Confronted at the outset with the loose integration of the widely dispersed parts of the university, he secured the appointment of a committee of national educational leaders consisting of presidents James R. Angell and Lotus D. Coffman of Yale and Minnesota, respectively; Dr. Arnold B. Hall of the Brookings Institution, with Dean George A. Works of Chicago as its agent, to study the organization of the university and to make recommendations for its development.

The formula to be followed was, to Chase's logical mind, comparatively simple even though the problems were exceedingly complex. Utilize the University Council as a Planning Committee for constant planning; appoint a provost to concern himself with instructional and financial programs; reorganize such units as could be re-

* *Ibid.*, pp. 3-4.
** This house was leased by the University from the Rhinelander estate. Later, an old Georgian brick house at 5 Washington Square, North, was leased from Sailors Snug Harbor and served as the Chancellor's residence for the remainder of Chase's administration.

IN A METROPOLITAN AREA 41

grouped advantageously; and, in due course coordinate and strengthen the administration of the various colleges or schools through deanships whose incumbents would largely assume responsibility for their efficient operation and steady upbuilding. At the time of his retirement eighteen years later, all of the deans of the university who administered its fourteen major units were appointees of Chase; and coordination and integration of a flexible nature remarkably adapted to the requirements of the institutional setting had been secured.

The nature of the task ahead of Chase was many-sided. Five matters, however, constantly loomed large before him. The first was enrollment. The number of students varied from approximately 32,523 in 1933-1934 to 70,376 in 1949-1950 following World War II.* If the 70,376 net enrollment for 1949-1950 (including summer school) had been divided equally among the 14 units, each dean would have had under his direction 5,000 students. The faculty for the two periods numbered approximately 1,700 and 4,000, respectively.

The second matter was finance. In the previous positions Chase had filled, the legislature was the principal source of funds. Student fees and tuition had to bear the brunt at New York University. At North Carolina and Illinois, the largest biennial maintenance budgets had been $1,730,000 and $12,280,000, respectively. At New York University, the beginning annual budget was

* Full-time students usually constituted approximately one half of the total enrollment. Data are from the *Report of the Chancellor.*

$7,018,760; the largest, in 1949-1950, $19,954,703, exclusive of the expenditures of the Medical Center.*

The third matter was physical plant. Various units were located at different parts of the city. Funds for new construction had to be found wherever they could be secured, from gifts, bequests, educational foundations, and city and Federal governments.

The fourth problem was that of extending and enriching the university's program of adult education. At North Carolina Chase had first actively participated as early as 1913, a decade before the establishment of The American Association for Adult Education, in the off-campus program of the Division of University Extension and later had strongly supported it as President. At Illinois he witnessed with enthusiasm the remarkably effective activities of the university and agricultural extension services. Consequently, in New York he looked forward with keen anticipation to the further development of the university's already extensive work in the adult educational field. This, he was convinced, was a peculiar function of an urban university, through which the educational and cultural interests of the public could be greatly deepened and enriched.

Difficult as these problems were, the fifth problem, that of building up the University in all departments and bringing it to membership in the Association of American Universities, was probably even more demanding of con-

* Data are from correspondence with Daniel D. Robinson, Controller, New York University.

tinuous thought and effort. To these tasks, Chase resolutely set his hand.

Each *Report of the Chancellor* for the years 1933-1934 —1950-1951 recorded the progress of the university in the solution of these problems. In looking back at the record at the testimonial dinner given in honor of him and Mrs. Chase by the Alumni Federation of the University at the Waldorf Astoria Hotel on January 24, 1951, Chase could visualize (as he had done in considerable detail in his *Report* for 1949-1950) a long series of accomplishments. He could see how successful he had been in the performance of the task to which he set himself at the beginning of his chancellorship. He could swiftly review the way in which the five major problems which had confronted him at the outset had been dealt with.

Enrollment

He had guided the institution for seventeen and a half years during which its enrollment, though constantly varying, had increased from 32,523 in 1933-1934 to a maximum of 70,376 in 1949-1950. Large as the totals were, and subject as they were to the violent fluctuations of the period, enrollment had never gotten out of hand.

Finances

He had kept within his annual budgets which varied from $7,018,760 in 1933-1934 to approximately $20,000,000 in 1949-1950, not including the Medical Center expenditures of approximately $7,000,000. Of the recurring income, approximately 85 per cent was derived from student fees, tuition, and gifts; funds for buildings were secured principally from special sources, including individuals, bequests, foundations, and the government of the City of New York and the federal government. The list of contributors, including the organized alumni, steadily increased throughout the period, evidencing the increasing impact of the university upon the metropolitan community, the state of New York, and the nation.

Physical Plant

During his chancellorship, Chase had witnessed the erection of a number of buildings and the addition of the Law Center, as well as the acquisition of extensive properties adjoining Washington Square and the renovation of existing Washington Square buildings. These latter moves resulted in the elimination of the threat of deterioration of the Washington Square area and its restoration to dignity and charm. The new engineering and gymnasium buildings and the adaptation of the Shepard mansion and grounds as the Elmer Ellsworth Brown House for English Studies added greatly to the attractiveness of the campus at University Heights, and new buildings at Hofstra College at Hempstead on Long Island increased the facilities of that new institution for effective work first as a junior and later as a four-year liberal arts college.*

* Hofstra College was established in 1935 at Hempstead, Long Island, under the academic control of New York University, through the bequest of the Hofstra Estate by Mrs. Kate Mason Hofstra in honor of her husband,

The crowning achievement in physical construction at a cost of $50,000,000 was the projection of the New York University-Bellevue Hospital Medical Center with its Post-Graduate College and New York University Hospital on a four-block site on East River. This development, begun under Chancellor Chase's administration and participated in by a number of interests, with its integrated plan of medical teaching, care, and research, gave form to a pattern of medical training that today is of national significance.

Adult Education

In accepting the chancellorship of New York University, Chase had welcomed the challenge which the university offered, not only for training for leadership but for the general diffusion of knowledge in the metropolitan area through its varied facilities for promoting adult education. Through its dispersed location in the area, through its well-coordinated organization, and through its commitment to an extensive adult education program, the university afforded him the opportunity to meet this challenge realistically. The *Report of the Chancellor* for 1950-1951, the last year of his administration, gave abundant evidence of the many ways in which the entire university participated in the work in this field.

The Division of General Education, established in the

William S. Hofstra. It was known as Nassau College-Hofstra Memorial. In 1939, the independent Board of Trustees terminated the contract with the university, and in 1940, the college received an Absolute Charter from the Regents of the University of the State of New York.

first year of Chase's administration, was designated as a specific unit of the university to carry on this activity. Soon after its establishment, the division organized a comprehensive program of training for leaders and teachers engaged in the work of the numerous agencies of the region, and has constantly contributed in this way to the effectiveness of the movement. During the regular session of 1950-1951, it carried services of the university to the community in meeting needs other than those of students preparing for their future careers. It also served as one of the public relations arms of the university through the organization of special conferences, institutes, and short courses. It enrolled in the regular terms 8,615 individuals in adult education programs and aided the various divisions, colleges, and schools of the university in conducting twenty-four special institutes and conferences for organizations interested in subjects as varied as foreign languages, labor, Federal taxation, secondary school papers, junior high schools, attacks on American education, recreation and camping, developments in reinforced concrete, social meaning of business in an arsenal of democracy, marketing, retailing, business education, legal concepts, society and the older citizen, the United Nations, and international health problems.

The significance of the effort of the university to meet the needs, not only of adults through informal education, but those of part-time and evening students throughout the area, is attested in other ways. Of the total 49,895 students enrolled in degree-conferring divisions of the university in the regular terms of 1950-1951, 27,623 were evening students. Supplementing the regular course work, the staffs and facilities of all of the major units of the university, including the law and medical centers, were made available to the community through lectures, workshops, forums, institutes, conferences, and legal and medical clinics.

During World War II, the university also served an additional purpose affecting not only the metropolitan area, but the nation at large. In common with other colleges and universities, it placed its entire resources at the disposal of the government for training and other types of special service. Thousands of service men and women were housed in its dormitories and trained in its classrooms and laboratories and following the war, it received an overwhelming flood of returning veterans in its regular programs of study and research. In 1950-1951, the Institute of Physical Medicine and Rehabilitation, the first unit of the Medical Center, was erected, equipped, and staffed for the rehabilitation of disabled service men and women.

In addition to providing for the administration and co-ordination of these vast public services, through the deans, the staffs, and the facilities of the university, Chancellor Chase strongly supported the adult educational activities of the area by means of public addresses and membership on the boards of trustees of such institutions as Town Hall, the New York Public Library, the Metropolitan Opera Association, and the American Adult Education

Association. Through all these organizations, with their unparalleled resources and their thousands of community leaders and molders of public opinion, as well as through the university, he sought to bring about for those whom they served "fuller understanding and larger wisdom as regards the complex civilization of today and tomorrow."

BUILDING UP THE UNIVERSITY

The steady building up of the undergraduate, graduate, professional and research aspects of the university was not something that could be so clearly visualized as the transformation of the physical characteristics of the Washington Square area, the significant building program of the College of Engineering, the completion of the superbly equipped Law Center, or the beginning of the remarkable development of the Medical Center. Chase, however, kept this objective always in the foreground of his thinking. The Division of General Studies combined and increased the notable extra-mural and intra-mural courses of the university. The academic programs in the fields of the arts and sciences, business administration and related fields, and education were greatly expanded and strengthened at both the undergraduate and graduate levels. The specializations of the university in architecture, the fine arts, and journalism were intimately related to the work of architects, artists, and journalists, and to the almost unlimited resources of the city in those fields. The work of the School of Engineering was extensively developed, with 30 of its 1,133 graduate students and 47 of its faculty members engaged part-time in 1950-1951 in research on 51 projects having a contract value of over three million dollars. The Postgraduate School of Medicine established in 1948 concluded its second year of highly specialized training for 1,160 physicians and established itself as a national and international center for advanced medical study. Of the total number of students, 360 were from 40 states, and 106 were from 23 foreign countries. The Graduate Division of Public Service, established in 1938, enrolled 720 persons for training for service in the field of public administration and members of the faculty of the university as a whole delivered hundreds of lectures in 1950-1951 and rendered a wide variety of specialized services in the capacity of consultant or advisor to civic, state, national, and international organizations. The university libraries had also been placed under unified direction and greatly strengthened, and they contained 927,577 volumes and regularly received 6,657 periodicals.*

In these and other ways, the work of the university, especially that of the graduate and professional schools and the university press, constantly brought the university to the favorable attention of the scholarly world; and in 1949-1950 the university received the acolade of membership in the Association of American Universities. In this action, Chase saw the happy solution of the problem which challenged him at the outset, that, on the one

* The data are for 1950-1951, taken from the *Report of the Chancellor*, 1950-1951.

hand, of training the public in such a way as to enable it to cope more effectively with the problems that confronted it, and on the other, of fostering and encouraging individual progress in advanced study and research to the limit of the university's resources.

In his first report, 1933-1934, Chancellor Chase noted that of the university's departments which offered graduate study, fourteen had been designated in a report prepared by President R. M. Hughes of Iowa State College to the American Council on Education as "adequate," but none had been designated as "distinguished." By the admission of the university into the Association of American Universities and by his observation of the throng of graduate students from many states and foreign lands who crowded its graduate libraries and laboratories and special centers, he was doubly assured that this part of the "provocative" challenge that eighteen years before had "attracted" him to the university had been splendidly met.

EDUCATIONAL DIRECTION FOR THE TWENTIETH CENTURY

THE pattern of higher education in America during the first half of the twentieth century was shaped by many forces and individuals. Among the leaders who contributed most significantly to its formation, Harry Woodburn Chase held a prominent place.

The nature of his contribution is readily apparent. It was made principally as the chief administrator of three American universities located in the South, the Middle West, and the metropolitan area of New York, all possessing different traditions and serving different clienteles.

At North Carolina, where financial resources had been and still were limited and conservative points of view were held tenaciously, he introduced the scientific method of study in psychology and laid the foundation for a distinguished Department of Sociology and of what is now the oldest and one of the most distinguished Institutes for Research in Social Science in the United States. He led the way in North Carolina and the South in scientific study and research in the social sciences generally and directed the thought of the region away from its past to that of its present and future. At the same time he insisted upon the application of national instead of local and regional standards in all study and research. He set excellence in higher education at the national level as the goal of the university and stoutly resisted deviation from it.

As he surveyed the South broadly, he also recognized the lag in its development of facilities for the preparation of students in such subjects as business administration and journalism, as well as in the dramatic and fine arts, and set about the establishment and development of new departments and schools in those fields. He visualized the

South as destined to become industrially a rapidly developing area, and strove to provide expert leadership not only for its economic and social welfare, but for the deepening and enrichment of its cultural heritage which it had long possessed and to which it clung tenaciously.

Edwin R. Embree, President of the Julius Rosenwald Fund, writing in the *Atlantic Monthly* in June, 1935, declared that the South had no great university of the first rank. Howard W. Odum, appointed by Chase as the head of the university's Department of Sociology and Institute for Research in Social Science, had said somewhat earlier that of the five resources essential to the development of a region—physical, human, institutional, technological, and financial—the South had the first two in abundance. It was rich in physical and human resources, but it lacked the last three—universities and technological institutions, scientific and technological know-how, and money—with which to develop them.

The solution of these acute problems Chase recognized was to be provided through the development of soundly based and highly staffed graduate and professional schools, a library stocked with resources essential to undergird strong programs of graduate and professional study and research, and a scholarly university press through which to transmit the findings of their research to other scholars and to the public. In these respects it can well be said that Chase led the way as early as the 1920's for much of the rapid development which has occurred in the

South in these fields in the two middle decades of the twentieth century.

In North Carolina and Illinois he emphasized the necessity of building up strong self-reliance and intellectual honesty in students through the assumption of responsibility for student self-government. Later, in New York, he continued the fight for freedom to teach and publish begun against the fundamentalists in North Carolina and strongly opposed McCarthyism in the form of enforced subscription by teachers to anti-communist oaths. The former fight helped to defeat the nationwide movement to throttle scientific teaching, the latter to stiffen national opposition to a new form of intolerance.

As an administrator Chase made little claim to originality. He went about his administrative tasks quietly and unhurriedly, but he knew the value of expert direction. The School of Commerce* established by him at Chapel Hill in 1919 was one of the relatively early organizations in that important field, and at all three of the universities which he directed one of his first acts was to reorganize administrative structures in order to facilitate the fundamental programs of instruction, research, and public service. At New York University he called in experts not only at the beginning, but again later to assist in coordinating administrative and academic operations. At Illinois and New York he established councils or committees, somewhat similar to the Advisory Committee at North Carolina, whose principal responsibility was to

* Later designated the School of Business Administration.

promote short- and long-range planning for institutional development. This procedure, today taken for granted in educational and industrial organizations, had scarcely begun in 1919, and did not become a national movement until it was made imperative by the depression of the early 1930's.

A further recapitulation of Chase's activities at Illinois and New York is not required here. At both institutions frequent improvisation to meet rapidly changing conditions incident to depression, recovery, World War II, demobilization, and Korea, was inescapable. But during this period, and throughout the entire thirty-two years of his leadership in which two of the institutions directed by him were admitted to the Association of American Universities, his voice was constantly heard in the councils of higher and adult education of the nation in advocacy of measures by which the universities could better perform their tested functions and further advance the frontiers of knowledge and service. For Chase, membership in these organizations had great significance. Such association kept him in intimate contact with the educational and cultural thought of the day and enabled him to bring it to bear upon the aims and activities of the institutions which he administered. It likewise afforded him the opportunity to share with those bodies his experience and thought in the solution of problems in which his rarely equalled skill as an analyst, his knowledge of educational objectives, his wisdom in making decisions, and his proficiency in formulating policies for the implementation of decisions arrived at could be most advantageously utilized. In this way, and through his writings and addresses, the goals which he set for the advancement of education in the rural South, the agricultural and industrial Middle West, and the highly complex metropolitan North could be achieved and extended throughout the nation.

Although Chase spoke humorously on one occasion of the trials of the president of a university,* he never underestimated the opportunity which the presidency offered for significant personal service. He also recognized fully that it was the universities, in both peace and war, to which the nation must look in large measure for the maintenance of its democratic way of life; for the advancement of its knowledge and cultural attainment; and, in the final analysis, for its very survival. His conviction deepened that if the intellectual, cultural, and spiritual resources of men were to be further strengthened and if the struggle for the freedom of men's minds was to be won, dependence upon universities, public and private, was imperative. It was to the direction of such indispensable institutions that he dedicated the four most fruitful decades of his life.

* "The Troubles of a College President," March, 1932.

www.ingramcontent.com/pod-product-compliance
Lightning Source LLC
Chambersburg PA
CBHW031715230426
43668CB00006B/219